EXMOOR & DARTMOOR

CLASSIC COUNTRY COMPANIONS

EXMOOR & DARTMOOR

PHOTOGRAPHS BY SIMON MCBRIDE · COMMENTARY BY LYDIA GREEVES

FOREWORD BY

ANGELA RIPPON

PAVILION

*With grateful thanks to my father, Patrick Greeves, who lent
me his extensive library of Dartmoor books, and to my brother,
Thomas Greeves, who helped me research the text*
LG

First published in Great Britain in 1993 by
PAVILION BOOKS LIMITED
196 Shaftesbury Avenue, London WC2H 8JL

Text copyright © Lydia Greeves 1993
Photographs copyright © Simon McBride 1993
Foreword copyright © Angela Rippon

Designed by Andrew Barron & Collis Clements Associates

The moral right of the authors has been asserted

A CIP catalogue record for this book is available from the
British Library

ISBN 1 85145 977 4 (Hbk)
ISBN 1 85793 031 2 (Pbk)

Printed and bound in Singapore by Tien Wah Press

2   4   6   8   10   9   7   5   3   1

This book may be ordered by post direct from the publisher
Please contact the Marketing Department
But try your bookshop first

Page 1: Ponies on Sherberton Common, Dartmoor
Page 3: Wheal Betsy's engine house, Dartmoor
Page 6: One of the combes running north from The Chains, Exmoor
Page 9: The River Dart, Dartmoor
Page 10: The Oare Valley, Exmoor

CONTENTS

BEING A REPORTER FOR a local newspaper or television station in the West country has to be one of the best ways there is to get into the heart and soul of the place. You discover hidden hamlets and little gems of character and beauty that as a tourist, or even a native, you might never know existed. Every story takes you through landscape as varied and arresting as any in the land, and you meet people whose lives, accents and outlook on life are woven in the fabric of the West, as much as the green fields, craggy tors and characteristically windy, hedge-lined lanes. It's all there, every day of your working life . . . and you're actually being paid for the pleasure of enjoying it. At least I was during the ten years I was working on local newspapers, radio and television.

Because I was born in the city of Plymouth, Dartmoor was my backyard. A vast, glorious playground where we played rounders on summer Sunday afternoons with assorted uncles, aunts and cousins, surrounded by waist-high ferns, quietly-grazing ponies and the ragged outcrops of a dozen granite tors. Later, I ventured further by bicycle. Through primrose-clad lanes to valleys shaded by ancient oaks, where the stillness of the moor was overlaid with the sound of moorland streams rushing and gurgling over mossy boulders, and the shrieks of children paddling, or swimming in the icy cold pools. At 18 I bought my first car, a much-loved 1947 Austin Seven. By then I was a junior reporter, and armed with a note book, and later a tape recorder, I started to meet the real people of the moor. The weather-beaten turf-cutters, the soft-spoken shepherds who tended the shaggy, hardy moorland sheep. Women who had walked miles to school in all weathers every week day, then repeated the exercise at weekends carrying precious eggs and home-made cream or butter to market. But it wasn't until I started to ride that I really got inside the true spirit of the moor. To be able to take off on a fit, fast horse, and leave cars, roads and people behind, is still one of the greatest freedoms and pleasures of my life.

As a child I suspect that I took it all for granted. The clean air, the amazing sunsets over the bracken and heather, the seasons that smelt and looked different as they ripened from green to gold. The colours that changed landscapes from the fiery gold and burnished copper of Autumn, to the stark black and white of an etching under a cloak of February snow. But as an adult, I can't believe how lucky I was to grow up in a place which, almost by osmosis, has had such a profound influence on the way I think and my attitudes to, and appreciation of, the world in which we live. Since those early days as a young reporter I've been fortunate in that my professional life has taken me all over the world, so that now my memory banks are a collage of the sights, sounds and smells of five continents. But Dartmoor and Exmoor still remain special.

There really is nothing quite like walking or riding over springy moorland turf, listening to the skylarks singing while they hover in a big empty sky. Or seeing a stag's head emerge suddenly from bracken, laced with early morning mist. Feeling a clean, sharp wind tug at your hair on top of a granite tor with the panorama of fields and villages, and dry stone walls stretching away to the horizon. In her text Lydia Greeves sums up exactly what I feel about Dartmoor and Exmoor, while Simon McBride's photographs capture the very essence of this ancient, wild and lovely landscape. Every river, every view, every skyline is an old friend.

So is this book a true representation of the two moors? Let's just say . . . It makes me feel very homesick!

Angela Rippon

WHENEVER I DRIVE WEST, back to the Dartmoor village where I spent much of my childhood, my heart lifts as soon as I leave the M5 motorway at Exeter and set out on the slow, winding road to Moretonhampstead and the moor. Just before the pretty village of Dunsford, a few miles out from Exeter, the route crosses the boundary of the national park and the road plunges into the deep groove of the Teign valley, running for a couple of miles through the oak woods that shade the river here. All the time, you are climbing, up to a saddle over the 1,000-foot ridge through which the Teign has cut so deeply. Then it is down, foot poised over the brake as the road careers headlong into the Moretonhampstead valley, snaking wildly round sharply-angled bends and with field gates in the hedges offering tantalizing glimpses of the moorland scenery ahead.

Moretonhampstead itself, a bustling market town on the fringes of the moor, is a delight, with a row of seventeenth-century almshouses and a powerful church set high on a hill. For me, it is the gateway to Dartmoor proper. Up to here, the road has been running through the encircling 'in-country', a pastoral hill and valley landscape of small fields and high-banked lanes, scattered with farms and villages. Beyond the town, it begins the ascent to the high moor. Hedges, fields and the intimate cosiness of the in-country are left behind in a starkly beautiful landscape of vast distances and wide horizons, with not a house to be seen.

Dartmoor is one of the wildest of Britain's ten national parks, a huge extent of haunting, untamed country where, even at the height of summer, it is possible to walk for hours without seeing another human being. Rising to over two thousand feet above sea level, it is the highest land south of the Pennines, with rocky, fast-flowing rivers that can rival anything to be seen in Wales or the Lake District. The centre is a gently-swelling, peaty plateau, most of it over 1,500 feet, with blanket bog covering many square miles of what, in driving rain or swirling mist, can seem frighteningly featureless country. The most dramatic, colourful scenery is round the edge. Here, where the purple moor grass and bog cotton of the badly-drained tops shades into a girdle of heather and bracken moorland, deeply-gouged, wooded valleys, many of them gorge-like in their steepness, cut far into the hills. Fingers of farmland stretch tentatively into the moor, with stone-walled fields climbing up the gentler slopes between spurs and tongues of rough, open grazing on the higher land. Above rise the jagged, rocky outcrops known as tors, where the underlying granite breaks through in fantastic, weathered shapes, some suggesting the ruined battlements of a medieval castle, others more like some huge, sleeping creature. Many tors are surrounded by a loose jumble of boulders known as clitter, broken off the main mass of the rock by the freeze-thaw action of frost.

Granite is the key to the moor. The boundaries of the national park, enclosing a heart-shaped area some 15 to 18 miles wide by 20 long, roughly trace the edges of the great boss of igneous rock which underlies the whole region. Granite has shaped the natural landscape and has been used since the Middle Ages to build Dartmoor's attractively rugged farms and hamlets, the narrow hump-backed bridges and the sturdy churches, and to wall lanes and fields. Thousands of years ago, when the climate was warmer and kinder than it is now, prehistoric peoples settled these uplands, dragging the moorstone boulders into the enigmatic rows and circles that bring a frisson of something primeval and unfathomable to the hills, building stone-footed huts and burying their dead in the round, grassy humps known as barrows, or in the rectangular pit-graves known as cists, like stony chests sunk in the ground. Although no one monument can rival the grandeur of Avebury or Stonehenge, Dartmoor's prehistoric remains are the most extensive in Britain, and their grand and lonely setting is unrivalled.

When the climate began to worsen, around 1500 BC, there was a gradual retreat from the higher land, and the pattern now is of a sparsely-populated centre with a cluster of towns and villages round the edge. Over the centuries, though, the moor has continued to play a vital role in the local economy. Fringing parishes radiate out from the heartland like the spokes in a wheel, the green lanes that twist up from the valleys once used to drive flocks and herds to the valuable summer grazing on the tops. In Norman times, the high central plateau became a royal hunting ground, but all of Devon had what were known as commoner's rights on the unenclosed land beyond the boundaries of the forest. There was hidden wealth here too, with many now lonely valleys once ringing to the sound of pick and shovel and the clip-clop of pack ponies as medieval miners searched for the rich deposits of tin that they hoped might transform their lives. Mining continued into modern times, reaching a high point in the later nineteenth century, but the miners have all gone now, their workings reduced to grassy and heathery humps and scatters of wall. Only the forest remains, its acres today forming part of Prince Charles's Duchy of Cornwall estates.

Dartmoor fills the belly of Devon. On the county's northern edge, lying across the border with Somerset, is Exmoor, also a national park but smaller, lower and more melodious than its counterpart to the south. For a start, it is underlain, not by granite, but by more conformist slates, grits and sandstones, which outcrop only rarely. These rocks have weathered into gently swelling hills, their heathery summits seldom above 1,400 feet. The highest point, 1,705-foot Dunkery Beacon, rises on the eastern side of the moor, where the view sweeps over the lush oasis of Porlock Vale and the wooded combes which cut deep into the uplands. This is the charm of Exmoor. Except in the bleak country known as The Chains, where expanses of grass-covered blanket bog echo the peaty heights of Dartmoor, the tops are broken up by sheltered valleys, some a sea of oak woodland, others with villages and farms set among green fields. Indeed, on the eastern side, Exmoor is positively fractured, with prominent valleys detaching the Brendons and the Selworthy ridge above Minehead. To the north, the hills run straight into the sea, forming some of the most glorious cliff scenery in Britain. Here you can walk for miles along the sheep-grazed, wind-swept, hump-backed ridge that follows the coast, most of it rising over a thousand feet above the sea, with a long steep fall plunging into vertical cliffs. West of Porlock, the coast is wooded, with trees almost down to the beach and a remarkable series of cliff waterfalls, where short, torrential streams leap headlong to the shore.

Inland, wide horizons are unexpectedly softened by farms. As on Dartmoor, the heartland became a royal forest, where the deer and other animals were reserved for the king, but this Crown land was disposed of in 1819, when some 10,000 acres were sold to one John Knight, the man who is largely responsible for Exmoor as it is today. Knight was a man of his age, an entrepreneur and improver who set out, like the better-known Coke of Norfolk, to make 'two blades of grass grow where only one grew before'. Perhaps, too, he was fired by the same imaginative spirit as his illustrious relative Richard Payne Knight (1750–1824), who left a fine collection of coins and bronzes to the British Museum. As a start, John Knight built a wall right round his estate, sections of which still stand, and he employed two hundred Irish labourers to make an enigmatic seven-acre lake in The Chains. More importantly, he spent a small fortune on reclaiming vast tracts of moorland, and built roads to link Simonsbath, the capital of his enterprise, to Exford, Lynmouth and South Molton, routes that now form the main arteries across the moor. His son Frederic carried on the good work, building farms, planting windbreaks, and working out how this unpromising land could be successfully cultivated. Much earlier settlers have also left their mark on the moor, but the prehistoric remains here are less numerous and more subtle than those on Dartmoor.

Both parks have much to offer. Popular spots such as Dartmoor's Burrator Reservoir, a picture-postcard, tor-girt lake, or Exmoor's Doone country, where thousands make the pilgrimage to the wild moorland combe that inspired R. D. Blackmore's romance, are much visited, even crowded at the height of summer. But those in search of solitude can always find it. For me, the best memories are of long July days on the moor, the air gloriously fresh, a faint breeze cooling the heat of the sun, a lark singing high overhead, and with a heathery slope to sink into at midday.

Lydia Greeves
January 1992

EXMOOR

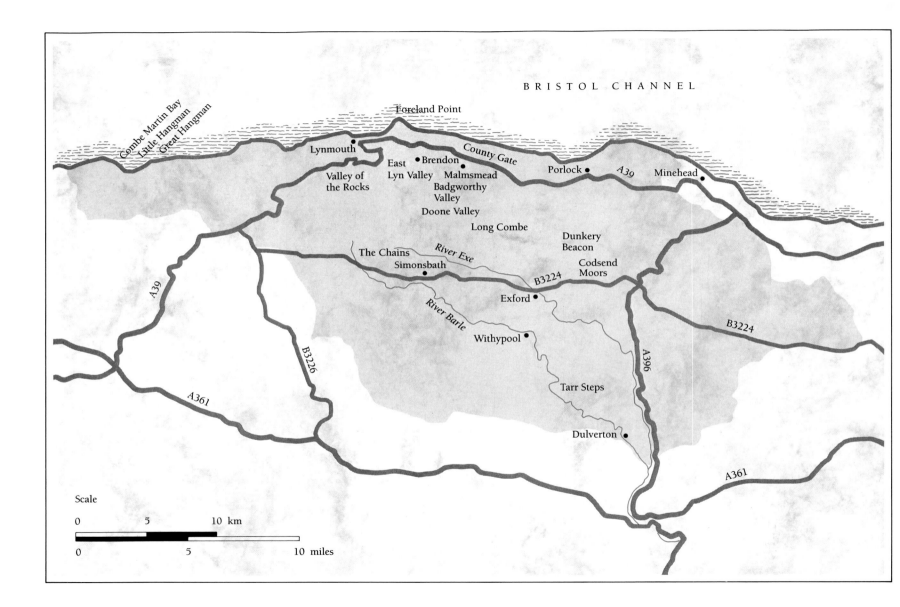

BRISTOL CHANNEL

Combe Martin Bay
Little Hangman
Great Hangman

Foreland Point

Lynmouth

County Gate

East
Lyn Valley

Brendon

Malmsmead

Porlock

A39

Minehead

Valley of
the Rocks

Badgworthy
Valley

Doone Valley

Long Combe

Dunkery
Beacon

The Chains

River Exe

Codsend
Moors

Simonsbath

B3224

River Barle

Exford

B3224

A39

Withypool

A396

Tarr Steps

B3226

Dulverton

A361

A361

Scale

0   5   10 km

0   5   10 miles

Exmoor is the moor of the Exe, the long river which rises in the high plateau country on the west side of the national park, only a few miles from the coast, and then flows east and south, right across Devon, to a wide estuary on the English Channel. Here, it has left the moor and is running through a broad valley above Tiverton, the town where R. D. Blackmore, author of *Lorna Doone*, went to school.

One of the southern approaches to Exmoor is along the deeply cut valley of the River Barle. Sometimes this is no more than a slot between precipitous, wooded slopes; sometimes there are lush meadows fringing the water, with grazing sheep and cattle. One of the few roads crossing the moor follows its lower reaches, and this valley cutting deep into the high hill country seems to have been a route for Iron Age man too. Prominent, wooded hill spurs, half-moated by the winding river, are crowned with the banks and ditches of prehistoric hill-forts, among them Oldberry Castle above the little town of Dulverton, and Mounsey Castle and Brewers Castle two miles upstream.

This ancient stone walkway stretching 120 feet across the River Barle is the finest clapper bridge in England. Curiously known as Tarr Steps, which may be a corruption of the Celtic *tochar*, a causeway, the bridge is roughly made, with great slabs of local gritstone forming seventeen 'arches' over the water. Sloping stones like primitive cutwaters strengthen the piers on the upstream side, but the bridge sits so low over the river that sections are likely to be swept away in times of flood. A deep ford runs beside it, but there is no other bridge here, the nearest crossing points for motorists being several miles up and downstream.

Probably built in medieval times, Tarr Steps was an important link in the system of ancient trackways crossing the moor, and must often have carried strings of packhorses, stepping sure-footedly across. Today, the laden ponies have been replaced by walkers. Paths run up and down valley from here, and Tarr Steps is on the route of the Two Moors Way, the long-distance footpath which cuts right across Devon.

During the summer months Exmoor's wild ponies need to build up the fat reserves that will see them through the winter. The true Exmoor is a strong, sturdy beast, a direct descendant of the herds which roamed these hills in prehistoric times, all senses tuned to detect the wolves which preyed on the young and the weak. Pure-bred stock has been much diluted by cross-breeding, but the black tails and oat-mealy muzzles of this little group suggest they may be true Exmoors.

Withypool, set among green fields, is an unexpectedly pastoral oasis in the depths of the moor. The village clusters on the north bank of the Barle, looking down on the six-arched, nineteenth-century bridge spanning the river and across the water to the swelling domes of the Common and Withypool Hill, with a stiff climb to the prehistoric barrows and stone circle crowning their summits.

About two miles above Withypool is Landacre Bridge, a five-arched, roughly-built old structure carrying the road from Exford to North Molton over the Barle. Upstream are the high moors feeding the headwaters of the river, and the few fields still fringing the water are framed by gorse and bracken-covered slopes. Fortunately, the Exmoor Society managed to defeat a scheme to build a reservoir in this wild and beautiful valley.

Except in the very bleakest parts, there are patches and pockets of cultivated land all over Exmoor, with several farms on land over a thousand feet above sea level. Many of these, and the beech hedges which shelter fields and lanes, were the creation of the enterprising Frederic Knight, whose father John had bought 10,000 acres of Exmoor Forest from the Crown in 1818 and set about putting what had been open moor under the plough. The estate is now fragmented, but the farms Frederic created survive, their acres now largely devoted to raising beef cattle and sheep.

The wildest, loneliest stretch of Exmoor is The Chains, a boggy plateau-like expanse rising to almost 1,600 feet on the west side of the forest. In the middle, filling a depression in the uplands, is Pinkworthy Pond, a desolate triangular lake formed by damming the headwaters of the Barle. Created by John Knight, it is the strangest of the improver's enterprises, neither beautiful nor useful, and often shrouded in swirling mist. Not surprisingly, the pond is said to be haunted, by the ghost of a young farmer who drowned here in 1889.

The rain-soaked bogs of The Chains feed the headwaters of the Exe, Barle, Hoaroak Water and West Lyn, the steep-sided valleys of the streams carving deep into the central plateau. The writer Henry Williamson used to wander this country, and enjoyed lying stretched out on the grass in summer, as if drawing inspiration from the ground. His Tarka came here too, sleeping in rushes by Pinkworthy Pond during the day, and once watching a stag 'hastening with tongue-a-loll' from the hounds and horsemen at his back.

In the soggy moorland of The Chains, unwary walkers risk sinking to their knees in the deep pockets of peaty bog between the tussocks of coarse grass. Because of an impermeable pan of iron just below the surface, it is wet even in mid summer, with tiny rivulets threading in every direction. Over this unyielding ground, on the night of 15–16 August 1952, broke one of the most violent rainstorms ever recorded in Britain. The water, unable to soak in, poured off the moor in angry, boiling torrents, the streams coalescing to form the catastrophic flood which descended on the fishing port of Lynmouth, mowing down everything in its path and sweeping cars and boats far out to sea.

The combes running north from The Chains are grassy at their heads, but are covered in bracken, heather and clumps of gorse as the valleys deepen. This is the kind of country where you are likely to see buzzards hovering silently overhead and hear the bubbling song of the curlew, or catch of glimpse of the white rump of a wheatear.

In the Bronze and Iron Ages, when the climate was drier and kinder than it is now, Exmoor was home to groups of hunters and herdsmen. Prominent summits carry the banks and ditches of hill-forts, ridges are crowned with the enigmatic humps and outlines of round barrows, and there are a few clusters of hut circles. This striking, saucer-like disc, the boundary of a circular enclosure, lies in the glorious walking country north of Lynton, where the moor is broken into deep combes by the Hoaroak, Farley Water and West Lyn.

Watersmeet, where the Hoaroak Water joins the East Lyn in a gorge-like wooded valley, is the centre of some of the most dramatic and beautiful country on Exmoor. Both rivers are fast-flowing, while above them wooded slopes soar hundreds of feet to the crests of the combes, with outcrops of bare rock and great slides of tumbled scree breaking the blanket of trees. The grey arch of Chiselcombe Bridge, for foot traffic only, spans the East Lyn just below Watersmeet, where the river swings round in a horseshoe bend to flow east to Lynmouth. The water looks angry enough here, but in the 1952 flood it was high enough to sweep the bridge away. Just upstream, where the two rivers join, is a homely, early nineteenth-century fishing and shooting lodge. This whole area, an estate of some 1,500 acres, is now owned by the National Trust, and the lodge has been converted into a tea-room, shop and information centre.

A quiet stretch on the Farley Water, which runs north to the sea on the east side of Cheriton Ridge.

A precipitous path off the A39 leads down to Watersmeet, where boiling cataracts and waterfalls along the East Lyn and Hoaroak Water are a major attraction. Canoists carry their fragile boats down from the road to chance their luck among the rapids.

The sheltered, deeply-cleft valleys of the Lyn, Hoaroak and Farley Water are known for their flora, with rich growths of lichens, ferns and mosses thriving in the damp, clean air, so close to the sea. One of the rarest plants is the Irish spurge, *Euphorbia hyberna*, known in mainland Britain only at Watersmeet and one other site.

Another cataract on the Hoaroak Water. These north-flowing rivers tear headlong to the coast, descending over a thousand feet from their headwaters high on the moor.

A typical Exmoor drystone wall, beautifully constructed of rough, local 'rag'. Stone-faced banks are also common, and many roads and fields are framed by neatly clipped beech hedges.

Trees grow tall and straight in the valley woodlands, where the soil is deepest and where plants of all kinds are sheltered from the biting spring breezes that can quickly chill anyone venturing out on to the tops. Near the crest of a combe, woodland becomes low and stunted, and out on the hills the trees planted as windbreaks have been warped and bent by the westerly gales.

The Trust's estate at Watersmeet is criss-crossed with some thirty miles of footpaths, some of them broad tracks, others scrambles over rough ground. Many of the paths are old donkey and mule tracks, once busy with animals bringing out timber and charcoal. Every twenty-five years or so the trees would be coppiced; stripped bark was used in the tanning industry, while poles became fences or hurdles, or were shipped across the Bristol Channel to the coal-mines of South Wales, to be used as pit props. A hundred years ago, anyone walking through these woods would have seen smoke from charcoal-burners' fires spiralling up among the trees.

The dramatic scenery of the cleave country was 'discovered' in the nineteenth century. The twenty-year-old Shelley brought his teenage bride, Harriet Westbrook, to a cottage in Lynmouth in 1812, during their wanderings after a scandalous elopement; the poet Robert Southey, who described this stretch of north Devon as 'an English Switzerland', and a host of well-to-do visitors in search of romantic scenery, soon followed.

The walk down the East Lyn, lyrically described in Murray's *Handbook* for 1879, is little changed, with a succession of picturesque footbridges leading from one bank to the other, and cool woods overhanging pools and boiling rapids. The fast-flowing stretches of the river are the places to see dippers, their white throats briefly visible as they bob in and out of the stream, and the inappropriately named grey wagtail, with its lovely lemon-coloured breast and tail.

The valley woods around Watersmeet are largely of sessile oak, but keen-eyed naturalists will be able to pick out scattered specimens of the rare Devon Whitebeam, *Sorbus devoniensis*, and its close relative, *Sorbus subcuneata*. Some slopes are richly carpeted with bluebells, there are trout and salmon in the rivers, and red deer are occasionally glimpsed among the trees.

The valley of the West Lyn is the most precipitous of these northern streams, descending 1,500 feet in four miles. The name Lyn itself means a torrent, from the Saxon, *hlynna*, and both branches of the river funnel down to the sea through ravine-like valleys.

The harbour at Lynmouth, a tiny slot carved out of the fast-flowing channel carrying the East and West Lyn to the sea, is backed by precipitous wooded cliffs rising to over a thousand feet above the port. Herring fishermen used to put out to sea from here, and moorland farmers enriched their acid land with lime from the eighteenth-century kilns that still stand on the quayside, once fed with Welsh limestone brought across the Bristol Channel on sailing ketches. Before this coast was 'discovered' in the nineteenth century, there was very little building here, and there is just one terrace of picturesque old cottages, climbing steeply up the cliff along the old track to the harbour.

The first hotel was built in Lynmouth in 1807, and during the nineteenth century the little town continued to develop steadily, with houses stretching back along the river. On the terrible night of 15–16 August 1952, when torrential rain on the high moors sent millions of gallons of water roaring down the gorge-like valleys which converge on the town, many of these buildings were destroyed or damaged beyond repair, and 34 people lost their lives. Since then, the town has been resurrected, and improvements made to control the course of the river.

Lynton, Lynmouth's other half, sits high up above its sister town, cradled in a hollow in the cliffs. This is an unashamed late-Victorian and Edwardian holiday resort, a place of barge-boarded, gabled villas, with some fancy tile-hanging and Gothic turrets. The key to Lynton's development was the building of the cliff railway that still joins the two towns. For years, the punishing gradients on the cliff road had deterred all but the most determined visitors, who were forced to walk or make the perilous ascent on the back of a donkey. The railway changed all this. Built in 1890 and largely financed by the publisher George Newnes, it is gravity-driven, with the weight of water in a tank beneath the descending car used to haul the other car, its tank emptied, up a nearly vertical track. In the early years, the railway would also transport motor cars that were not powerful enough to cope with the bends and gradients on the cliff road.

From the high, hog-backed cliffs running east to Foreland Point there is a splendid view of the headland above Lynmouth, with the stony beaches at the mouth of the Lyn forming a dark fan against the glistening waters of the bay.

A spectacular cliff path from Lynton, with views to South Wales across the Bristol Channel, leads a mile or so west to the Valley of the Rocks. This strange, streamless combe runs parallel to the coast, separated from the sea by a craggy, jagged ridge with deeply-jointed beds and blocks of rock piled up in unlikely, suggestive shapes. Filling the end of the valley, like some scaly, prehistoric creature about to leap into the sea, is Castle Rock, a steep-sided outlier of the main ridge. Not surprisingly, the valley caught the romantic imagination of Shelley, Wordsworth and Coleridge, and Victorian visitors regarded it as one of the wonders of the West Country. The rock-strewn valley is thought to be a legacy of the Ice Age, when sea-ice blocked the path of north-flowing rivers and forced them into this narrow corridor. This view, taken from the seaward side of the ridge, shows Castle Rock rearing up against the sky; beyond it, on the nearer headland, is a folly tower.

The landward side of the Valley of the Rocks is a steep, bracken- and gorse-covered slope, with a scatter of substantial boulders. Hidden among the rocks there may be some of the wild, white goats that live in the valley, and the animals are sometimes seen high on the seaward crags, theatrically silhouetted against the sky.

A single-track toll road running west from the Valley of the Rocks leads to this splendidly-sited mansion looking over a grassy sward to the sea. Although called Lee Abbey, and entered through a defensive, Gothic-arched gatehouse, there is nothing monastic about it. Most of the building, including a fanciful octagonal music room with huge traceried windows that forms a chapel-like bay in the middle of the west front, dates from 1850, when an older manor house was much enlarged. A folly tower crowns Duty Point, the wooded triangular promontory to the left of the abbey, and directly behind it is the high, distinctive profile of Castle Rock.

The only approach to the wild and atmospheric Heddon Valley is down narrow lanes like green rabbit-holes. The road stops at the much-frequented Hunter's Inn, with a touch of the Black Forest about its half-timbered gables, and from here an easy path leads on a mile or so down the combe. At first, the way is through oak woodland framing an open floor, but towards the coast the valley closes in and becomes more dramatic, its steep sides bare with expanses of scree or blanketed in gorse, bracken and heather. Martinhoe Beacon, the hill swelling above the valley to the east, carries the banks and ditches of a Roman look-out point, manned for about twenty years in the first century.

At its mouth, the Heddon emerges into a secluded rocky cove, its eastern side framed by the bold headland of Highveer Point, with bare cliffs rising steeply from the water. Just above the pebbly beach, like a romantic eyecatcher, are the remains of a lime kiln, once used to process limestone brought in from South Wales. Little boats also landed Welsh coal here, and there is a long tradition that they carried more exciting cargoes too, such as the 96 casks of brandy said to have been brought ashore one night in 1801. This is one of the most beautiful and unspoilt stretches of the north Devon coast, with spectacular views from the cliff paths, west to Widmouth Head on the far side of Combe Martin Bay and east to Foreland Point.

The bracken-covered pyramid known as the Little Hangman rises 716 feet above the evocatively-named Wild Pear beach, on the east side of Combe Martin bay. Beyond – out of the picture – is the Great Hangman, a brooding mass of a hill over a thousand feet high which can look positively sinister in the dusk of a winter afternoon. Both hills are splendid viewpoints, with wide vistas inland towards the heart of Exmoor. In summer, skylarks sing high overhead, and there are wheatears and stonechats to be seen.

Above Lynmouth, the main road west to Porlock climbs almost a thousand feet up formidable Countisbury Hill, emerging on the crest of the hogback ridge which gives this coast its magnificent cliffs. The two-mile incline is pretty tough going even today, and in the days of horse-drawn traffic the coach journey from Lynmouth to Minehead took three hours. This country is dramatically beautiful at any time of year, but can seem particularly majestic under snow, when walls, trees and isolated farm buildings stand out starkly black against the surrounding whiteness.

East of Combe Martin is the natural harbour of Watermouth Bay, a long square-ended slot running inland for about half a mile. It is much frequented by the sailing fraternity and usually crowded with little boats.

The hamlet of Countisbury, with the grey tower of St John's church rising above a little cluster of cottages, sits just below the crest of the hill. The sixteenth-century Sandpiper Inn by the side of the main A39 is a favourite stopping point and rendezvous for walkers, and was once a staging post for the horse-drawn coach service between Lynmouth and Porlock. Above the village is rounded Butter Hill, topped by the mast of a television relay station, and beyond it a path leads on a mile or so to Foreland Point. This peaceful, sunny scene gives no hint of the nightmare conditions that can sometimes be experienced along this coast, as on the stormy night in January 1899 when the people of Lynmouth, unable to launch their lifeboat, hauled it for eleven hours over the hills to Porlock so they could go to the aid of a stricken ship.

East of Lynmouth, Exmoor meets the sea in precipitous, 900-foot cliffs, exhilarating walking country with well-trodden paths leading out to the lighthouse on Foreland Point, the most northerly headland in Devon. West of Countisbury, a steep, zig-zag path, for the sure-footed only, leads down to golden Sillery Sands, but most of the shoreline is inaccessible. The Foreland is bare and sheep-grazed, but to the east, in the lee of the promontory, oak woodland clings to the cliffs, coming right down to the shore in places, and shades the coast path, which runs on, undisturbed by any road, for miles. This is red deer country, and herring gulls, kittiwakes, shags, guillemots and other seabirds ride the winds, their cliff nesting colonies safe from almost all predators.

Hundreds of feet below the open cliffland at Countisbury, but only a mile or so south as the crow flies, the village of Brendon lies buried deep in the valley of the East Lyn. A river walk west from here, much of it through woodland, leads to Rockford, with its welcoming inn, and on to Watersmeet and the deep cleave that drops down to Lynmouth.

Moor farms are almost always built into hollows in the hills, sheltered from winter gales. Typically, the older houses are long and low, with walls two or three feet thick and protective porches shielding the entrance. Everything is of local stone, more difficult to work than the granite of Dartmoor, but serviceable enough. The wall in the foreground is traditionally constructed, with rough courses of uncemented, uneven stones capped with a fringe of flat stones set end on, like jagged teeth.

On the A39 coast road, the point where Devon rolls over into Somerset is marked by County Gate. To the east, on the Somerset side, is Yenworthy Common, where these sheep are foraging beneath the snow. Any animal pastured on the moor needs to be hardy and resilient, able to last out the winter if need be, and it is the traditional hill breeds, such as the Cheviot and Exmoor Horn, that are most likely to thrive.

The pastoral landscape at the northern end of 'Doone country', which runs south from the coast on the border between Devon and Somerset. Narrow, high-banked lanes, sparkling streams, ancient farms, deep, secluded combes and the wild heather moors all fed R. D. Blackmore's imagination, and he wove the places he knew into his romance.

The tiny village of Oare, with its gabled manor house set back into the hill and the church of St Mary almost hidden by trees. This is where Lorna Doone came to be married to John Ridd, in 'a dress of pure white, clouded with faint lavender', and where she was shot down at the altar by the villainous Carver Doone. Strangely, fact merges with fiction. There have been generations of Ridds in the parish, and Blackmore's Farmer Snow was based on the family who once lived at the manor. St Mary's itself, where Blackmore's grandfather was rector from 1809 to 1842, is a modest, rough-built country church, filled with box pews. Lorna's assailant is said to have aimed at the wedding couple through one of the narrow Gothic windows just west of the screen.

From Yenworthy Common, one of Exmoor's steep lanes leads down to the little village of Oare, here barely distinguishable among the snowy fields.

Below Oare, the infant East Lyn flows in a great loop through a deep-cut wooded cleave. Although only a mile from the coast here, these sheltered valleys are protected from the gales which sweep over the open moorland of the cliffs. Coming down into them from the coast road, the roar of the wind is replaced by a sudden quietness.

As petrified tree stumps found in peat diggings have shown, Exmoor was once probably almost entirely forested, even on land well over a thousand feet above sea level. Most of the open country has long been cleared, but the mixed woods clothing the steep-sided cleaves are one of the glories of the moor. This wintry scene is in the Oare valley.

No road leads to the isolated combe from which the outlawed Doones are supposed to have terrorized the surrounding countryside, and those intent on seeing the supposed ruins of their dwellings must walk a couple of miles up the valley from Malmsmead, the hamlet below Oare. With its hump-backed bridge spanning the Badgworthy Water, its paved ford, and the long whitewashed building known as Lorna Doone Farm, Malmsmead is a picturesque spot, but is best seen in the winter, when there are fewer visitors about. For much of its length, the stream marks the county boundary, with one bank in Devon, the other in Somerset.

The Badgworthy valley runs directly south, cutting deep into high, bare moorland. Although well trodden by parties of Doone pilgrims, the combe still feels secluded and becomes increasingly wild once the meadows and farms around Malmsmead are left behind, with bracken and heather-covered slopes closing in on either side. For the walker, despite some rough scrambles across side-combes, the path is easy enough, little more than a gentle ramble. Often, the way runs through woodland, most of it oak, but with the occasional stand of fir. The only blot on the landscape is *Rhododendron ponticum*, the wild rhododendron, which lines the stream in places and is sadly invading heathery slopes.

The old woodland of gnarled oaks that shades the path to Doone valley. On the northern flank of the wood, the Badgworthy Water is joined by the Lank Combe, a lovely, rocky moorland stream that may have inspired R. D. Blackmore's watery barrier guarding the entrance to the Doone's lair. Only those with imagination, though, will be able to transform the combe's gentle falls into 'the long pale slide of water . . . faced on either side with cliff up which the young John Ridd scrambled so perilously, reaching the top half-drowned and with his legs knotted with cramp.

The path to Hoccombe Combe, the high side valley about two miles up Badgworthy Water where the Doones had their lair. Here, grass- and bracken-covered ruins suggest the rough, single-storey stone houses either side of the stream which Blackmore describes. Although the crumbling walls are in fact the remains of an originally medieval settlement, possibly inhabited by a small community of hermits, Blackmore's romance was inspired by tales of the desperadoes who are believed to have terrorized Exmoor in the seventeenth century, and who may well have gone to earth in the combe.

In *Lorna Doone*, Hoccombe Combe is described as 'carved from out the mountains in a perfect oval, with a fence of sheer rock standing round it, eighty feet or a hundred high; from whose brink black wooded hills swept up to the skyline'. As the many who flock here discover, this scene-painting owes rather more to imagination than the truth, but there is a desolate grandeur about the sweeping grass and heather moorland around the combe, with panoramic views for those who climb up out of the valley and take a high-level route back to Malmsmead.

A twisting, single-track road follows the upper reaches of the Oare valley, eventually climbing out of the combe to join the main A39 up a hair-raisingly steep hill with a couple of fearsome bends. Here, the road is crossing the stream at Robber's Bridge, a popular beauty spot.

The Weir Water valley, one of
the headstreams of the East
Lyn, joins the Oare above
Robber's Bridge.

The path through Weirwood,
in the Weir Water valley.

Approaching Exmoor from the east, through the colourful, lively village of Porlock, motorists are faced with one of the steepest hills in Britain. From Porlock, which is only a few feet above sea level, the main A39 west to Lynmouth rises 1,350 feet in under three miles, climbing up and up, with spectacular views of the sea and back over Porlock Vale. At the top is the bleak, heathery expanse of Porlock Common, with a Bronze Age stone circle beside the minor road running south to Exford.

Together with the Scottish Highlands, Exmoor is one of the last safe haunts of the shy and beautiful red deer, the largest of Britain's wild mammals. Visitors to the moor rarely see them, as they tend to lie up in bracken and woodland during the day, only coming out in the evening. This herd on Porlock Common, about a dozen animals in all, is typically small, with several fawns in among the hinds and antlered stags. When born, these calves have dappled coats, like fallow deer, only turning to the characteristic ruddy brown after the first three or four months.

On the east side of Exmoor, the National Trust's huge, 12,500-acre Holnicote estate includes some of the most glorious country in the area, with lovely walks up wooded combes that rise steeply to open moorland. The network of paths, many of them with delightfully eccentric names such as Cat's Scramble, or Granny's Ride, dates from the time when this whole area was owned by the Acland family; rides and tracks on the Selworthy Hills were even regularly swept clean by old-age pensioners. This scene is near Luccombe, one of four estate villages now largely owned by the Trust.

A well-used track snakes to the horizon on the heathery expanses of Codsend Moors, sloping gently down from Dunkery Beacon.

In the heart of the moor, grassland interrupted by peaty hollows undulates towards distant horizons.

A wooded valley near the little village of Cutcombe on the east side of the moor is known for its winter display of snowdrops. The stream is flowing north, towards the Bristol Channel, but in this watershed country around Wheddon Cross there will be a south-flowing river just across the hill.

The only significant peak on Exmoor is Dunkery Beacon, the highest point, whose heathery slopes rise 1,705 feet above the sea. Visible from miles away, Dunkery was used as a signalling point for centuries, with a supply of firewood kept ready on the summit for lighting the beacon. In recent times, fires have been lit to celebrate such special events as the Coronation, or Royal Weddings. Although high, the Beacon is not difficult to reach, with easy paths to the summit from the road between Dunkery Gate and Luccombe.

Panoramic views from the top of Dunkery Beacon look over the rolling border country and the sea of foliage in the wooded combes cutting deep into the moor. A northerly stance, and a less misty day, would reveal Porlock Bay and the coast of Wales across the Bristol Channel; the Brendons and Quantocks are clear to the east; while, to the south-west, the higher tors of Dartmoor, and even Brown Willy on Bodmin Moor, fifty miles distant, can be seen on the horizon. As the photograph makes clear, this slice of north Somerset is enchantingly unspoiled, a picturesque mix of farmland, woodland and open moor.

The view of Dunster Castle, rising high on a steep wooded mound at the mouth of the Avill valley, delights all who drive past on the coast road to Minehead and Porlock. This Camelot-like vision, with its towers and battlements, is in fact largely nineteenth-century, a romantic reconstruction in local red sandstone by the Victorian architect Anthony Salvin. No trace remains of the Saxon fortress built here, or of the Norman keep which once crowned the tree-covered hill behind the house, but a fifteenth-century gatehouse (on the right) still straddles the steep approach from the village, and beside it, although not visible in this photograph, is a thirteenth-century gateway. Home of the Luttrell family for six hundred years, the castle is now owned by the National Trust, and open during the summer season.

Dunster Castle towers over the little village at its feet. The steep approach up Castle Hill, past the Luttrells' seventeenth-century stable block, debouches into the main street of the village, a charming ensemble of old stone and timber-framed cottages. Early prosperity was built on cloth-making, and one of Dunster's most photographed buildings is the octagonal yarn market of 1589 in the village square. Once, too, there was a Benedictine abbey here, but all that remains of the priory is a round dovecote, a sixteenth-century barn and the splendid church of St George, with its Tudor screen and Luttrell monuments.

The medieval pack-horse bridge which crosses the Avill below Dunster Castle, a ford close beside it.

The ancient, two-arched Gallox Bridge over the Avill is much used by walkers and riders heading for the wooded paths on the opposite bank.

Some of the best views on
Exmoor are over the moorland
fringe, where high hills, covered
with grass and heather, melt into
the pastoral landscapes of north
Devon and Somerset.

DARTMOOR

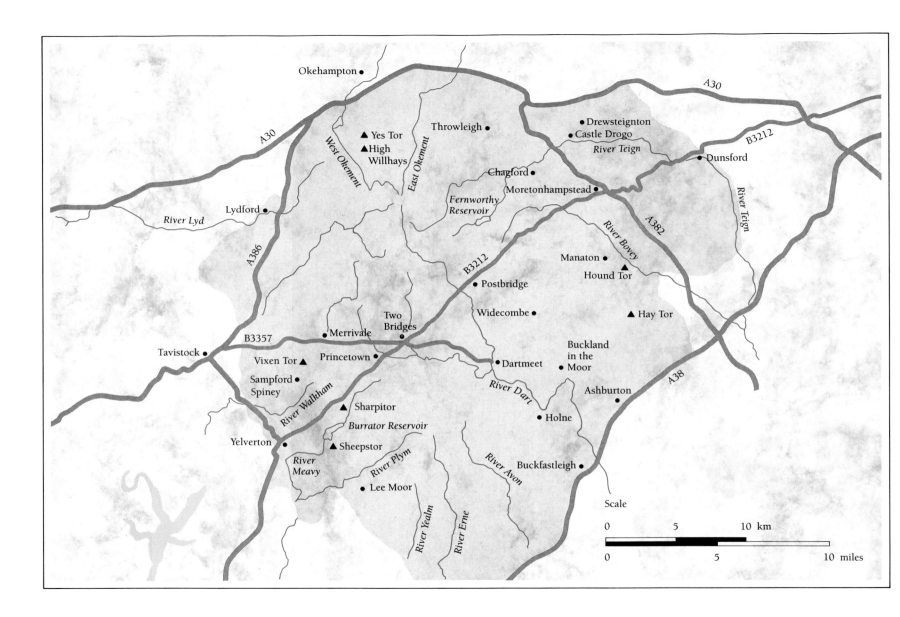

Burrator Reservoir, a much-visited beauty spot, lies on the south-west edge of Dartmoor, folded among the hills. Forestry plantations ring the water, and side valleys, the headwaters of the drowned River Meavy, cut deep between the surrounding tors. Completed in 1898, Burrator was the first reservoir on the moor, built to serve the increasingly thirsty town of Plymouth. Above the lake, and on Roborough Down nearby, are the leats which used to supply the port, the earliest of them promoted by Sir Francis Drake in the sixteenth century. This view, taken from Yennadon Down on the west side of the reservoir, looks across the water to Sheepstor. Toward the head of the lake, beyond the low, wooded peninsula projecting from the right bank, is the dramatic rocky profile of Leather Tor, with the pyramidal peak of Down Tor over to the right. A road circles the reservoir and leads to the tiny village of Sheepstor, burial place of the extraordinary James Brooke, Rajah of Sarawak, who returned from the East Indies in the 1850s to end his days on a local estate.

Inside one of the conifer plantations at Burrator. All this woodland is owned by the Water Authority, who took over the whole Meavy catchment area after the First World War. The farms in the headwater valleys had to be abandoned, their sites now marked by crumbling ruins.

The southern side of Sheepstor is a jumble of the fallen granite blocks known as clitter, where the unwary could easily twist an ankle. Below the tor is one of Dartmoor's most spectacular Bronze Age stone circles, with four rings set one inside the other, and the hill in the middle distance, above the patch of trees, is rich in the remains of nineteenth-century tin mining, including the huge pit dug to take a fifty-foot diameter water-wheel.

The valley of the Plym above Cadover Bridge, where the river meanders across a broad, grassy flood-plain, is one of the softer landscapes on the moor and a favourite haunt of picnickers and summer paddlers. In the distance, above the farm on the slope of the hill, are the rocky piles of Trowlesworthy Tors. All is peaceful and serene, but just out of the picture rise the chalk-white spoil heaps of the Lee Moor china clay works, whose activities are transforming this area of the moor into a cratered moonscape.

Huckworthy Bridge over the Walkham is reached through a web of narrow, high-banked lanes. An old mill, now converted into a house, sits by the bridge, and upstream from here is a wild and beautiful wooded valley.

This moody evening shot looks over the wooded Walkham Valley to gentle Pew Tor, silhouetted on the crest of the hill. The fields below the tor surround the remote village of Sampford Spiney, with a church dating back to the fourteenth century and an ancient manor-house, now a farm. It was through this splendid country that the Plymouth to Princetown railway once ran, curving round the rocky mass of Ingra Tor in the foreground.

The impressive, sphinx-like lump of granite known as Vixen Tor stands high over the Walkham valley beyond Pew Tor. Rising over ninety feet from the ground, this is the tallest rock mass on Dartmoor and also one of the most disturbing, with the deep joints in the stone easily transformed into the outlines of animals and weathered faces. Not surprisingly, the tor has inspired legends and folklore, including the story of a witch who lures travellers to their death in the mire beneath the hill. This view looks across the head of the valley to Sharpitor, with the line of the Yelverton to Princetown road cutting cleanly across the slope of the hill.

The only granite quarry still working on Dartmoor is at Merrivale, where the spoil heaps just stop short of the main road from Two Bridges to Tavistock. The loose granite boulders known as moorstone have been used by man since the Bronze Age, but it was only in the nineteenth century that the first quarries were opened, the strong, resilient stone being used for such landmarks as Nelson's Column in Trafalgar Square, the British Museum, and Dartmoor prison, which is just up the road from Merrivale. The scattered houses seen here are the remains of the mining village which developed round the quarry at the end of the century. Some impressive abandoned workings surround Foggin and King Tor to the south of this road, where giant blocks of half-dressed stone are lined up by the side of the access track like a piece of landscape sculpture.

The Merrivale road runs through one of the richest concentrations of prehistoric remains on Dartmoor. There are hut circles and enclosures, cairns, the stone-lined, box-graves known as cists, and traces of reaves, the prehistoric equivalent of boundary walls. Particularly memorable are the three stone rows to the south of the road, the longest stretching 865 feet across the moor and two of them consisting of double lines of boulders. This splendid menhir, which stands slightly apart from the rows, is over ten feet tall.

This rather forlorn row of cottages high on the moor was built as part of a Victorian enterprise that had the personal blessing of Prince Albert. To the right of the photograph, in the wooded valley of the Cherry Brook, are the evocative ruins of a water-powered gunpowder works, among them sturdily built grinding houses, a couple of lonely chimneys and the remains of the leat system which fed the water-wheel. This terrace was where the foreman and manager lived, the latter occupying the rather larger house with a projecting porch in the middle. Until it was superseded by dynamite in 1867, gunpowder was used for blasting in the tin mines and stone quarries, and was taken by horse-drawn wagon from here to the slate quarries at Delabole in Cornwall. Producing such dangerous and volatile material, which was tested on site, the works had to be isolated, and this remote moorland valley was the ideal location. One of the workers used to eat both his breakfast and his dinner early in the day, in case he was blown up later on.

A bleak wintry view from above Postbridge, with Bellever Tor rising out of a sea of conifers on the horizon. These plantations, part of extensive afforestation in the inter-war years and immediately after the Second World War, caused considerable disquiet, with many people fearing that the character of the moor was being changed for ever. The serried ranks of trees, though, have enriched Dartmoor's bird population, providing breeding habitats for the merlin, chiffchaff, redpoll, nightjar, coal tit and gold crest.

This fine clapper bridge over the East Dart at Postbridge was probably built in the thirteenth century to carry the medieval track between Chagford and Tavistock. These primitive constructions, with great slabs of granite laid across rough, uncemented piers of piled-up boulders, continued to be built up to the nineteenth century, and there are several examples on the moor. Postbridge, nearly 43 feet long, is the largest, its central arches carried eight feet over the river. The little roadside settlement at this point is a much later development, dating from the late eighteenth and early nineteenth centuries, when this area of the moor was first enclosed.

Bellever Tor from the south-west, the only direction from which the hill does not appear ringed by trees. Vast tracts of the central moor are covered by hummocky grass, an inhospitable, sepia waste in the winter months.

Off the much-used main road from Princetown to Moretonhampstead, the south-eastern wedge of the moor is crossed by an enticing web of lanes, some of them unfenced, others sunk between walls and hedge banks. This road runs south from Postbridge, with the remains of another medieval clapper just visible to the left of the three-arched bridge over the East Dart.

The moor is a moody sort of place, where sunshine can transform the landscape. To the right of this road across Cator Common, clearly visible on the skyline, are the ridge and furrow corrugations caused by ploughing, evidence that the moor was once more widely cultivated than it is now.

No signpost points down the narrow, stone-walled lanes leading to Jordan, a picturesque hamlet hidden away in the wooded West Webburn valley. Among the buildings clustered above the stream here is this enchanting old manor-house, its thatched roof sweeping low over the upper storey and a single block of granite forming the arch of the projecting porch. Although much altered, this sturdy, weather-worn farm dating from the seventeenth century is a splendid example of the long, low buildings dug into the hills that appeared all over the moor from medieval times. Jordan was one of the Dartmoor manors mentioned in Domesday, and at one time was the focus of a 1,260-acre estate, with extensive grazing rights on the hills. Like many other places round the moor, it had a share in the profitable cloth trade which brought Devon so much wealth in the fourteenth to sixteenth centuries; just down the road from the house stands the manor water-mill, most recently used for grinding corn, but once engaged in processing the coarse, short wool from the estate's Dartmoor sheep.

Although now converted into a separate dwelling, this roughly-built house with a splendid granite doorway was once the barn attached to Jordan manor. The door opens straight on to the little stream running through the farm, with a slab of granite forming the bridge across.

Dartmeet, where the east and west branches of the River Dart meet in a deep wooded valley, is one of Dartmoor's most popular beauty spots. One of the two main roads over the moor, that from Ashburton to Tavistock, crosses the river here, with notoriously steep, relentless climbs up the slopes of the valley on either side. Those who walk away from the huge car park beside the bridge can find sheltered picnic spots on grassy banks, dark, enticing pools, and boulder-strewn stretches, where the river is a race of boiling water. The actual confluence of the two rivers is downstream of the bridge, while beside it are the rather forlorn remnants of a medieval clapper, largely destroyed in a flood in the early nineteenth century.

These days, all kinds of animals may be seen pastured on the moor, from llamas to donkeys. Few, though, are tough enough to withstand the winter without help.

The Walla Brook, which flows into the East Dart above Dartmeet, marks the eastern boundary of the Royal Forest for much of its course. There are three Walla Brooks on the moor, their names thought to be derived from the Old English *weala,* meaning Welsh or foreigners, a reference to the Celtic peoples who once inhabited these uplands.

The elegant arch of the late eighteenth-century bridge across the West Dart at Huccaby, built high enough to withstand the floods that swept away its predecessor. Downstream, beyond the bridge, the valley closes in, channelling the river down to Dartmeet through Huccaby Cleave. Just upstream from here, the West Dart is joined by the Swincombe, a little moorland stream that rises in the boggy shifting ground of the notorious Foxtor Mire, a place of exhilarating desolation.

Dartmoor is named after the great river which flows 46 miles south and east to the Channel from sources at about 1,800 feet in the highest, north-western section of the moor. Whereas most other rivers tentatively reach out into the moor, the Dart boldly crosses it, forcing both the main roads across the centre to bridge it at least twice. Here the river has left the high moor, and is flowing through the pastoral country that rings it on all sides.

These rough stone cottages by a narrow hump-backed bridge are near Holne on the south-east fringes of the moor. Many buildings such as these have been sympathetically restored in recent years.

A long with many other traditional crafts of the moorland area, thatching has seen a massive revival in recent years, with many houses and cottages now sporting freshly renewed roofs.

In the Middle Ages, three great abbeys flourished on the fringes of the moor, at Buckfast, Tavistock and Buckland Monachorum. Buckfast was the richest Cistercian monastery in the south-west of England, its wealth largely based on sheep farming and the wool trade, with connections as far afield as Florence. Initially founded before the Norman Conquest, and at one time affiliated to the Savigniac order, Buckfast's period of greatness dated from 1147, when it was taken over by the Cistercians. Like all other religious foundations, it was abandoned at the Dissolution, but, incredibly, there is again an abbey here. A group of Benedictine monks from France acquired the site in the late nineteenth century and started the restoration of the abbey, following the plan of the ancient buildings wherever they could. Their new church, 220 feet long, was built by the monks themselves, working under a master mason. Consecrated in 1932, it is now the centre of a living, working monastery. This photograph shows the abbot's chair.

These thatched cottages at Buckland in the Moor lie deep in a sheltered combe, down the hill from the granite church. The wall in front, dotted with ferns, channels a little stream which joins the gorge-like valley of the Dart about a mile downstream, in the depths of the oak woodlands of Holne Chase. Holne itself is where Charles Kingsley, author of *The Water Babies*, was born on 12 June 1819, while his father was curate-in-charge of the parish.

The best way to see Dartmoor is to walk, either striding across the tops or threading your way through the lanes that criss-cross the border country. Green tunnels such as this, lined with mossy stone walls, are a constant delight. Sooner or later the lane will climb steeply upwards, with wide views through field gates, or swoop downwards to cross a narrow, hump-backed bridge, with a sharp bend just before the stream.

From the right angle and in favourable light, any tor can be made to look dramatic. The little heap of Bonehill Rocks, here silhouetted against the smooth contours of Hamel Down behind, lies above the East Webburn valley and the village of Widecombe. Within easy reach of a road, it is popular with summer visitors.

Sheep have been grazed on the moor for centuries, and large monastic flocks attached to the abbey at Buckfast were pastured here in the Middle Ages. Today, northern breeds, such as the Blackface and the Cheviot, have largely displaced the true Dartmoor, which is a white-faced sheep. These three contented animals are sitting on one of the smaller granite outcrops on Saddle Tor; behind them are the rocky outlines of Bell Tor, Chinkwell Tor and Honeybag Tor, with the undulating, 1,700-foot ridge of Hamel Down on the horizon.

There is something elemental and primeval about the brooding mass of Hay Tor, whose two rounded granite bosses rising to about 1,500 feet above sea level are perhaps the most impressive rock outcrops on Dartmoor. Standing right on the edge of the high country, Hay Tor is visible for miles around, and its distinctive profile can even be seen from far out in the English Channel. This view is from Saddle Tor, only some twenty feet lower and almost as powerful.

As this view shows so clearly, the climate of Dartmoor is noticeably harsher than that of the fringe country. Snow is common in winter, frequently cutting off the more isolated farms, and often the heights will be white when the border country is free of snow. In the severer blizzards, falls can be heavy enough to bury stock alive. A storm in 1891 even enveloped a train on the Plymouth to Princetown line, covering the engine up to its funnel.

The compact, durable granite of Hay Tor was extensively worked in the nineteenth century, with no fewer than five quarries operating on the northern slopes below the tor. Here, the ground is pitted and scarred with the remains of spoil heaps and with the deep gouges of the workings, the most impressive of them a ravine-like gorge running back into sheer granite cliffs. Even more striking are the surviving sections of the unique granite tramway that was built to take the stone to the nearest shipping point, some ten miles away and 1,400 feet below the level of the tor. At its moorland end, the tramway branches again and again, sending smoothly curving arms into each of the main workings. Even the 'points' are made of granite, although they are now without the movable metal pieces that once deflected the trucks on to the right line. Sadly, this magnificent piece of engineering, with its embankments and cutting, had a busy life of only a few decades, from 1820 to the late 1850s.

The eastern side of the moor has a wealth of impressive tors, many of them standing high above deeply-incised valleys. This misty outline, like the ruins of a long-forgotten Crusader castle, is Hound Tor. The fantastic shapes of this granite mass, where the deeply-jointed rock has been transformed into pillars, bastions and battlements, have inspired any number of images and stories, including a vision of a spectral hound.

As this panorama westwards shows, Hound Tor is a good viewpoint. On the south-eastern slopes of the hill, overlooking the wooded valley of the Becka Brook, are the evocative remains of a deserted medieval village, with the clear outlines of three long houses and a number of other farm buildings among prehistoric and medieval fields.

Below Hound Tor and the attractive village of Manaton, where the novelist and playwright John Galsworthy lived for several years, the Becka Brook cascades over a great heap of jumbled boulders some thirty feet high. There is a short walk through mixed woodland to this much visited spot, and a longer, more attractive path leads on downstream to Lustleigh Cleave, where the River Bovey flows through a dramatically steep-sided wooded valley.

The village of North Bovey from the south-west, with the tower of St John's church forming a prominent landmark. The River Bovey is buried in the valley beneath the village, while a mile or so away, down a heart-stoppingly narrow lane, is the mock-Elizabethan manor of 1906–7, complete with hall and minstrel's gallery, that was built for the W. H. Smith family; it is now a hotel.

North Bovey's thatched
cottages are grouped around
a spacious green, which is rather
curiously planted with oaks, as if
the houses were enclosing a
wood. The village pump stands in
one corner and a granite cross,
not visible in the picture, in
another.

All over the moor, valleys are marked with the spoil heaps and gullies left by medieval tin miners. Incredible as it may seem today, in the second half of the twelfth century nearly all Europe's tin came from south-west Devon, and there was a second boom in early Tudor times, at the turn of the sixteenth century. At first, the miners worked the rich alluvial deposits along the upland streams, but as this tin became harder to find they began to follow lodes in the parent rock, gullying back into the hillsides in an early version of open-cast mining. In the nineteenth century new techniques, such as the use of explosives and pumping equipment, fuelled another boom, allowing the recovery of ore from far underground. Unlike the surface workings of medieval times, the Victorian mines involved shafts, drainage tunnels, huge, water-powered wheels to operate the machinery, and all sorts of surface buildings. Now, all has returned to the moor, with grass and heather-covered ruins where once there were scenes of frantic activity. These gullies are part of the extensive workings of the Birch and Vitifer Tor mine at Headland Warren.

As well as being one of the best areas in which to see the workings of medieval and more modern tin miners, Headland Warren is also an example of one of Dartmoor's rabbit farms. At several places on the moor, from the thirteenth century onwards, large areas of land were devoted to breeding rabbits, with artificial banks known as 'buries' mounded up to encourage them to burrow. Periodically, dogs would be used to drive the rabbits into netted areas, when the catch would be killed and taken to market on pack-horses or donkeys. The blizzard of 1891 which buried the Plymouth to Princetown train also dealt a severe blow to the warrens, killing off many of the rabbits. Most of the farms never recovered, and Dartmoor's last warrener died in 1969. Here at Headland Warren the miner's gullies made ideal rabbbit country. The little thatched building half hidden in the depths of the valley is the old warren house, with a rabbit-proof enclosure in front of it where the warrener grew hay. In the nineteenth century, when the mines were again being worked, an enterprising warrener turned the house into an inn, offering cider and beer and 'rabbits to eat'.

There are primitive granite crosses all over the moor. Most of these crude crosses are medieval, some erected to guide travellers across the moor, others to mark important boundaries. Bennet's Cross, shown here, is one of the most easily seen, standing as it does beside the main road from Moretonhampstead to Princetown, about a mile north-east of the Warren House Inn. Unusually, this cross has served more than one purpose. Most recently, as shown by the initials WB roughly cut into one of its faces, it has been a boundary marker, flagging the north-west extent of the great rabbit warren which stretched south of the road here (WB = Warren Bounds). When originally erected, though, it is more likely to have been a waymark, showing where the trans-Dartmoor track from Moretonhampstead met one from Chagford crossing over into the Widecombe valley. The most evocative of these medieval routes runs some nine miles across the southern moor, from Holne to Burrator.

The silvery glint of water in Green Combe demonstrates what anyone living on Dartmoor knows: this is one of the wetter places in Britain. When not being lashed by the westerly gales which bring 60 to 100 inches of rain a year to the Princetown side of the moor, the hills are often enveloped in a soft, gentle mist which makes even the most familiar tor seem menacing and sinister.

In the 1930s, an increasing need for water to supply Torquay on the south Devon coast led to the damming of one of the headstreams of the River Teign, and the creation of this placid reservoir on the eastern edge of the moor. The contrast with Burrator could hardly be greater. Whereas the former is surrounded by dramatic tors, the hills around Fernworthy rise gently from the water, and the western end is buried in huge conifer plantations. In times of drought, some interesting features of the drowned valley are briefly exposed, among them a prehistoric stone circle.

The Forestry Commission has laid out a number of walks through the conifer plantations ringing Fernworthy Reservoir. Often, there will be waterfowl on the lake, which has attracted tufted duck, pochard, mallard, teal, moorhens and coots.

From the fourteenth century, four 'stannary' towns – Chagford, Tavistock, Plympton and Ashburton – acted as regional centres of the tin trade. Here, the tinners brought their ore to be assayed and taxed, and here they would purchase the provisions needed until their next trip off the moor. This little town, set on a hill rising steeply above the River Teign, is Chagford, still unspoilt despite its more recent development as a holiday centre. Modest houses, some of bare stone, others plastered, the earliest dating from medieval times, line the streets running away from the church and the central square, with its octagonal Victorian market house; and, deep in the valley, the Teign is crossed by a three-arched granite bridge built in c. 1600. Chagford is still an important local centre and is set in some of the most enchanting countryside in Devon, with a tangle of narrow lanes for the adventurous to explore.

A misty, early morning view on heather-covered Chagford Common, just south of Fernworthy Reservoir.

Another medieval cross, standing beside the lane leading down into Chagford over Week Down, once marked the route from Moretonhampstead and North Bovey and also flagged the way to church for people from the outlying farms of the parish. It was once suggested that the sturdy shaft, nearly seven feet long, could be used as a footbridge, but happily it has been left where it is. Chagford is deep in the valley behind the rounded, half-cultivated hump of Nattadon Common.

One of Chagford's many delightful corners.

133

A view from the fringes of the moor over the farmland of the in-country, the shadows cast by this low evening light emphasizing all the dips and hollows in the landscape.

The market town of Moretonhampstead on the eastern edge of the moor is dominated by the spacious fifteenth- and early sixteenth-century church of St Andrew. This is a vigorous country town, with many attractive houses and cottages along the narrow streets that converge on the irregular central square. Once an important coaching stop, Moretonhampstead was later the terminus of the only railway to serve this area of the moor; coaches and trains have all vanished, but a couple of the inns which once catered for their passengers still remain.

These thatched almshouses fronting narrow Cross Street in Moretonhampstead raise the spirits of anyone coming into town on the twisting back road from Exeter. As the date stone unequivocally proclaims, they were built in 1637, with shaped granite columns supporting an open eleven-arched arcade along the front. Although delightfully unpretentious, this is a relatively sophisticated building to find in such a rural backwater at this date, its rough-and-ready Renaissance detailing probably reflecting the taste of a rich patron.

Downstream of Chagford, the River Teign plunges into a wooded gorge that cuts right across a substantial range of hills, running seven miles east to the charming village of Dunsford, with its thatched, cob-walled cottages. Oak woods hang above the river, the open canopy encouraging a rich woodland flora and a good range of birds, including the lesser spotted woodpecker.

One of the most picturesque spots in the Teign gorge is Fingle Bridge, hidden deep in the valley below the village of Drewsteignton. Probably built in the sixteenth century, its low granite arches now span the river beside the popular Angler's Rest, a magnet for summer visitors, but upstream of the bridge the valley is much quieter. Much of this land is now owned by the National Trust, and there are well-marked walks beside the river or high on the shoulder of the hill, where the evocatively named Hunter's Path gives dramatic views over the gorge and of the Trust's Castle Drogo. There are fallow deer in the woods, and on the south side of the river a gigantic granite wall, nine feet high in places, encloses the deer park made by Sir John Whiddon in c. 1570, now a gloriously varied mix of gorse and bilberry, broom and bracken, with pockets of oak, ash and rowan among outcrops of bare rock.

High above the Teign gorge, like a well-ordered tor, stands Castle Drogo, the romantic, pseudo-medieval country house which Sir Edwin Lutyens built between 1910 and 1930 for the nouveau riche Julius Drewe, founder of the Home and Colonial Stores. This view, taken from the south-west, shows the big stone-mullioned windows lighting the dining-room and drawing-room, but round the corner the house is much more forbidding, with granite walls rising sheer and unrelieved from the bracken-covered slopes of the gorge. Inside, the contrast between Edwardian comfort and medieval austerity is even sharper, with vaulted, stone-walled corridors and a subterranean kitchen, top-lit as if gouged out of the rock, teamed up with an elegant, softly-coloured drawing-room, with pale green panelling hiding the harsh granite walls. Like much of the gorge, Castle Drogo is now owned by the National Trust, and is regularly open in the summer months.

A peaceful scene in the pastoral border country in the parish of Throwleigh.

Together with the East and West Okement, the Taw is one of the few rivers on the moor to run north, emptying into the Bristol Channel at Barnstaple rather than heading south to the English Channel.

Many of the walls and banks of the border country are hundreds of years old, with oaks, beeches and other trees rooted deep within them. Here, birds and other wild creatures can find shelter, and hidden nesting places.

Dartmoor mares foal in April or May, and unwanted animals will be sold at one of the pony fairs held at various places round the moor. Once the annual round-up was a spectacular affair, like a cattle drive in the Wild West, but the lack of demand nowadays, coupled with the fact there is no subsidy on ponies, means stock levels have been greatly reduced. Some animals are taken on by the trekking stables, from which long strings of ponies, often with rather nervous riders on their backs, set out across the moor; some are exported for breeding and riding; but many, sadly, are bought by the meat trade.

On the south-west edge of Okehampton, on a spur above the West Okement, are the ruins of what was one of the largest castles in Devon. Like the town itself, this was originally a Norman foundation, but it was completely rebuilt in c. 1300 by one Hugh Courtenay II, who incorporated some sumptuous living quarters within the defences. Beyond the walled approach from the outer gateway, a long narrow bailey lined with the substantial remains of a great hall and other domestic buildings slopes gently upwards along the ridge. At the highest point of the spur, crowning what was the steep-sided Norman motte, is a double keep. The wooded valley rises behind, and there are also trees among the ruins, their foliage shading the site over the summer months.

This is Dartmoor at its wildest, its most primeval, and – for those who respond to these wild open spaces – its most exhilarating. But this north-west corner of the moor, with the high points of Yes Tor (2,030 feet) and High Willhays (2,038 feet), is only sometimes open to walkers. Since the 1870s, large areas have been used as a military training ground, and some thirty thousand acres are still under the army's control, with red flags flown to keep the public away on firing days. Even when no live ammunition is being used, you are likely to see helicopters buzzing round the tors like angry wasps, and diminutive camouflaged figures creeping across these vast open spaces. No doubt it was training in country such as this that made victory possible in the Falklands War, but the continuing presence of the army in what is supposed to be a National Park has caused more controversy locally than almost any other issue. This photograph was taken to the east of High Willhays, looking north over the conical summit of East Mill Tor, the only sign of civilization being the belt of woodland surrounding East Okement Farm.

One of the more dramatic sights on the moor is the deep gorge gouged out by the River Lyd below the village of Lydford. Trees, mosses and ferns cling to the cliff-like walls of the ravine, while far below the river roars and foams over a series of ever-deepening potholes. A slippery, narrow, and sometimes vertiginous path clings to the side of the gorge and leads on downstream to the White Lady Waterfall, where a side-stream cascades ninety feet to join the Lyd. In medieval times, Lydford itself was a thriving, fortified tōwn, site of the Forest courts and the stannary prison, and seat of a Saxon mint. Now, it is jūst a shadow of its former self, but a more illustrious past lives on in its splendid castle, in the earthworks of the defences and in the grass-grown lanes preserving the grid of the early-medieval streets.

Another view of the bleak north-western quarter of the moor within the orbit of the military camp outside Okehampton. Henry Williamson brought his Tarka here, leading him up the headwaters of the Taw to the bogs and hummocks of the moor, and showing him the strange frozen world of an ammil, when light rain falling in sub-zero temperatures encases every sprig of heather, blade of grass and bracken frond in a sheath of ice.

Low, winter sunlight picks up every ridge and furrow in this steeply sloping field on the edge of the moor.

The shell of Wheal Betsy's engine house is a romantic reminder of Dartmoor's nineteenth-century mining boom. The steam-engine housed here, with a massive rocking beam pivoted on a specially strengthened wall, would have worked the mine's drainage pumps. Coal had to be shipped round the coast from South Wales, and the fuel first used here, as in some other Dartmoor mines, was peat, brought over the moor from workings around the headwaters of the Walkham.

Ponies are a familiar sight on the moor. For centuries, they were used as pack-horses, carrying wool, peat and other goods along rough tracks, and stepping sure-footedly across the clapper bridges. In the nineteenth century, these small, sturdy animals were sold away from the moor to work in the coal mines of Wales, the Midlands and the North, while a lucky few found themselves pulling small traps and governess carts.

Ponies have roamed free over the moor for centuries. The indigenous Dartmoor stock was strong and hardy, able to withstand the severest weather and to find food in the roughest country, but recent cross-breeding has reduced the animal's ability to cope with Dartmoor's winters.

In the past, granite was used for everything on Dartmoor, from feeding troughs and cider-presses to gateposts. Until the nineteenth century, when the first large-scale quarries were opened, people simply used the boulders that lie about all over the moor, roughly shaping them with wedges and axes and building them into their farms and churches.

Around the high, uncultivated land at the heart of the moor lies the in-country, an intricate patchwork of small, stone-walled fields threaded by narrow, high-sided lanes. This is quiet, secluded country, with villages folded in the hills and byways leading to remote farms.

Granite boulders cleared from the fields formed Dartmoor's characteristic drystone walls. Some are centuries old, but others date from more recent attempts to tame and cultivate the moor. Around Princetown, land is worked by men from the grim, stark prison that was built here in 1806 to take soldiers captured in the Napoleonic Wars. There can hardly be a more unsuitable place for a town or a farm: set on a high shoulder of land at a height of 1,430 feet above sea level, Princetown has an average rainfall of over eighty inches a year, is frequently fog bound, and is open to winds from every direction.

A reminder of what winter on Dartmoor can be like. Beautiful as this scene is, heavy snowfalls usually spell misery and death for the animals pastured on the moor.

I STOOD WITH MY back to the wind protecting the camera and tripod, trying to minimize any 'camera shake'. It was a bright, wild and unusually cold, early May morning and the moors were alive! Mountainous white clouds raced across the sky, crows were frantically flying nowhere and two Dartmoor ponies were having their own rodeo in a gully below me.

I was trying to photograph a hut circle on Gidleigh Common above Fernworthy Reservoir. The darting shadows from the clouds were causing havoc with my light readings. Suddenly the wind dropped, it was very quiet and everything seemed to stand still. I became engrossed looking through a lens waiting for the right balance between light and form. After a while, I stood up and as I did, I was struck on the nape of my neck by something cold. I turned and facing me was an awesome and totally unexpected sight. It was as if nightfall had closed in behind me and out of the darkness snow had already begun to settle barely fifty feet away. This was the Dartmoor that I was learning to live with.

I moved to Devon in 1979 and, having spent my childhood and early career in Africa, I was immediately drawn to the untamed nature of the two great moors. I started photographing on Dartmoor and Exmoor in the winter of 1979, not because I had a commission or even a long term project in mind – I just loved being there and taking pictures! No two days were the same so it was a continuous challenge to photograph from a technical point of view. Furthermore, there was something irresistibly magnetic about such uncompromising landscapes. There were no half-truths, one had to be bold when trying to capture the essence of the two moors.

It's always tempting, but usually counterproductive, to use a wide-angled lens when confronted with a landscape such as Dartmoor. The effect is to diminish the scale of the landscape unless there is something very striking or large in the foreground which enhances perspective. I find it is far better to use a small telephoto lens such as an 85mm or 105mm lens to bring in the features, and which also helps one to be more selective about what to photograph.

Another problem for the photographer is the enormous amount of sky on the moors! As with most landscapes, the skies are a vital component, but on the moors they are often a dominant feature and say as much about the land as any other detail. Many of the photographs I have taken on Dartmoor and Exmoor comprise two-thirds sky, and this is where the problem lies. The light reflected from the sky can often be two or three times greater than that reflected from the land, and unless great care is taken with light meter readings many shots will end up underexposed!

I usually take a tripod with me, but nothing too heavy as I often have to walk a few miles up and down rugged and boggy terrain! If it's a windy day, I hang my camera bag from a hook I have attached to my tripod and this gives it good stability. Another trick is to take a plastic carrier bag and hang it from the tripod with a few heavy stones in it! Because of the enormous changes in the weather on the moors, I always take a few rolls of fast and extra fast transparency film to experiment with, otherwise I tend to shoot mainly on Kodachrome 64 and Kodachrome 200 which are wonderfully balanced films for landscape photography. I have a backpack type camera bag with easy access to all cameras and lenses, which spreads the weight load evenly over my ageing and ailing back!

One final tip, always look over your shoulder every few minutes when walking over the moors – I've seen many a stunning shot behind my back!

Simon McBride
August 1992